NOW YOU CAN READ

ZOO ANIMALS

TEXT BY STEPHEN ATTMORE

ILLUSTRATED BY GRAHAM ALLEN

BRIMAX BOOKS • NEWMARKET • ENGLAND

Bob and Julie are at a zoo.
They are looking at a large sign.
It says that you must NOT feed the
animals. The keepers do that job.
Extra food will make the animals
fat and may make them sick.

Which way should they go first?
Bob wants to go this way and
Julie wants to go that way.
The map shows where all the
animals are kept. They find out
which is the best way to go.
Then they follow the signposts.

Bob and Julie are lucky. They can watch the keeper feeding the sea-lions. The bucket is full of fresh fish. The keeper throws a fish and the sea-lion catches it in its mouth. Sea-lions are noisy when they are hungry.

Look at this lion. His teeth give us a clue to the food he eats. The long teeth help him to tear meat.

Camels' teeth are worn down by chewing plants.

Some animals need special foods. Koalas only eat leaves from one type of tree.

Toucans use their huge beaks to eat fruit and insects.

Sometimes zoo animals become ill.
The zoo vet looks after animals
when they are ill or injured.
Look at the vet checking the
animal's teeth. The giant panda
did not eat its food this morning.
Its jaw is swollen. Perhaps it has
a broken tooth.

Young animals in zoos are always
popular. They are kept inside
until they are strong enough to
go outside. Look at the mother
kangaroo. She is keeping her baby
warm in a pouch. The keeper is
giving milk to baby pumas. Their
mother did not want to feed them.

Bob and Julie are watching the big bears. They are like cuddly teddy bears. But look at their big paws. They can do a lot of damage with their sharp claws. One of the bears is climbing a tree. It is looking for food. Brown bears also dig up worms and roots to eat.

In most zoos monkeys and apes are kept near to each other. Look at the monkeys swinging about from place to place. They move very fast. Can you see what sort of food they eat? Two monkeys are sitting together. They are helping one another to keep clean.

There is often a lot of water at a zoo. Many animals like to swim. Otters are very good swimmers. Look at the beaver making a home. It is called a lodge. The entrance is under the water.

Bob is laughing. The hippos are yawning. Maybe they are tired. The pool is very muddy. Hippos like to have a mud bath.

Cats like a drink after a meal. This tiger is lapping up the water. Most cats do not like swimming. But when it is hot the tiger likes to bathe.

Julie likes the Reptile House.
It is warm and damp inside. These
animals do not like cold weather.
The crocodiles are lying still.
Are they sleeping? Julie is
looking for the lizard. It is hard
to find. The colour of its skin
is the same as the rocks.

Bob likes the snakes. They slip
and slide around. Snakes are fed
once a week. It takes their bodies
several days to deal with a meal.
Look at the frog's big eyes.
Is it watching you? The turtle is
swimming round and round the tank.
These animals like water too.

The children are now at Pets'
Corner. Sometimes it is called
Children's Zoo. Here you can touch
the animals. Bob is holding
a small snake. It is safe to do
this. Do you think it feels slimy?

Who is riding on a camel? As the
camel walks, it rocks the rider
about. Is Julie looking happy?
The keeper is leading the camel.
What other animals can you see in
this part of the zoo?

The giant ostrich is taller than
people. It cannot fly. But it can
run fast. There is a hummingbird
in the next cage. It is tiny.
It flaps its wings very quickly.
The parrot is making noises that
sound like someone talking.

Some zoos have only a few types of
animal. The dolphins are diving
over a line. They can leap high
out of the water. They also like
making big splashes. The fish
below are kept in big tanks.
Look at all the bright colours.

Safari parks are like big zoos.
Animals are free to roam about.
People drive their cars through
the park. You must NOT get out or
leave a window open. One monkey is
on top of a car. The big cats do
not seem to notice the cars.

On the other side of the road are
some elephants. They do look big.
One elephant is spraying water
with its trunk. Can you see the
giraffes? They are eating leaves
from the top of a tree. Their long
necks help them to reach up high.

Can you name these zoo animals?
Which ones do you like best?